Woodbourne Library
Washington-Centerville Public Library
Centerville, Ohio

THE WORLD OF OCEAN ANIMALS
CRABS

by Bizzy Harris

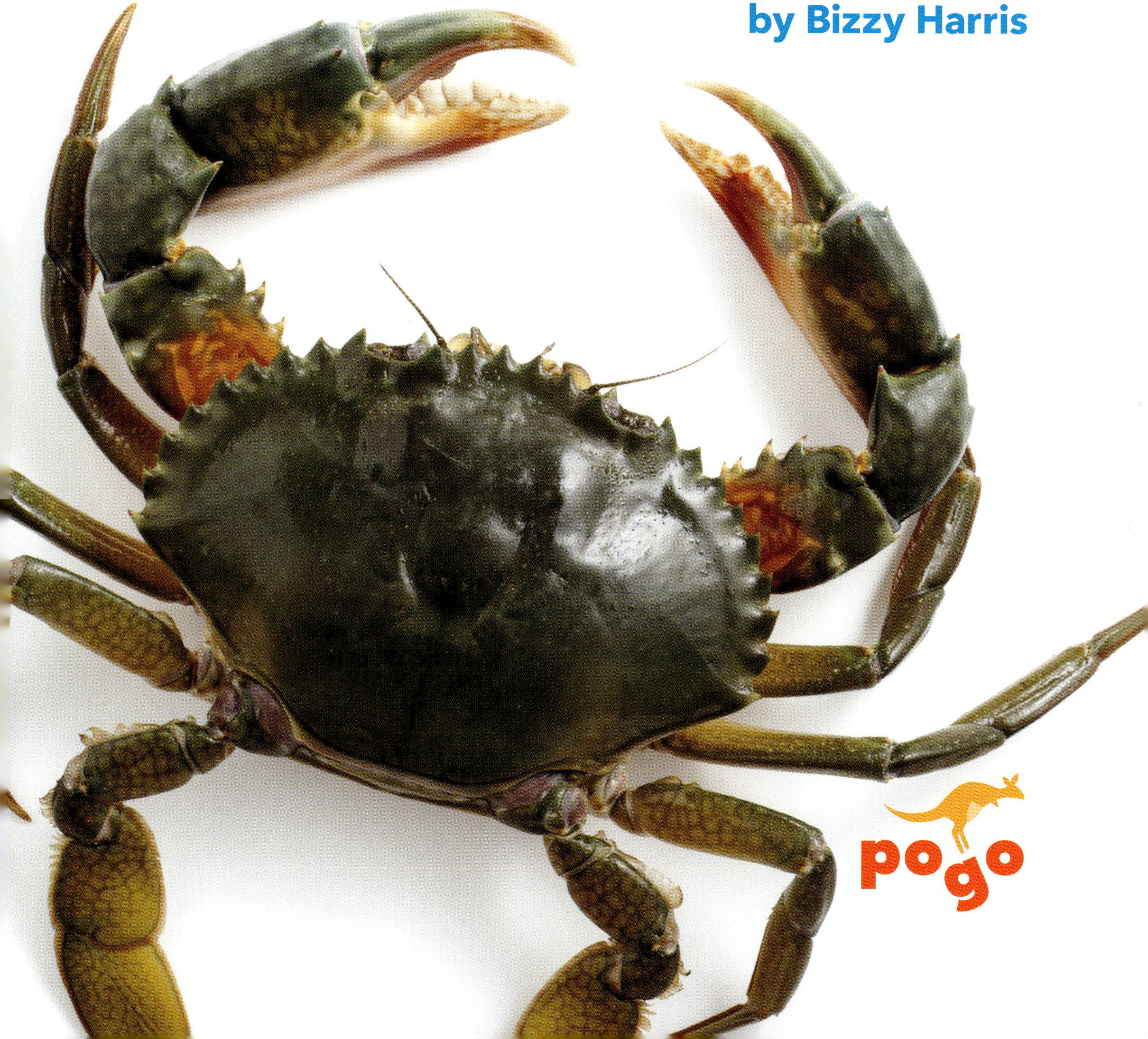

pogo

Ideas for Parents and Teachers

Pogo Books let children practice reading informational text while introducing them to nonfiction features such as headings, labels, sidebars, maps, and diagrams, as well as a table of contents, glossary, and index.

Carefully leveled text with a strong photo match offers early fluent readers the support they need to succeed.

Before Reading

- "Walk" through the book and point out the various nonfiction features. Ask the student what purpose each feature serves.
- Look at the glossary together. Read and discuss the words.

Read the Book

- Have the child read the book independently.
- Invite him or her to list questions that arise from reading.

After Reading

- Discuss the child's questions. Talk about how he or she might find answers to those questions.
- Prompt the child to think more. Ask: What did you know about crabs before reading this book? What more would you like to learn?

Pogo Books are published by Jump!
5357 Penn Avenue South
Minneapolis, MN 55419
www.jumplibrary.com

Copyright © 2022 Jump! International copyright reserved in all countries. No part of this book may be reproduced in any form without written permission from the publisher.

Library of Congress Cataloging-in-Publication Data

Names: Harris, Bizzy, author.
Title: Crabs / by Bizzy Harris.
Description: Minneapolis: Jump!, Inc., [2022]
Series: The world of ocean animals
Includes index. | Audience: Ages 7-10
Identifiers: LCCN 2021021718 (print)
LCCN 2021021719 (ebook)
ISBN 9781636902791 (hardcover)
ISBN 9781636902807 (paperback)
ISBN 9781636902814 (ebook)
Subjects: LCSH: Crabs—Juvenile literature.
Crabs—Behavior—Juvenile literature.
Classification: LCC QL444.M33 H36 2022 (print)
LCC QL444.M33 (ebook) | DDC 595.3/86—dc23
LC record available at https://lccn.loc.gov/2021021718
LC ebook record available at https://lccn.loc.gov/2021021719

Editor: Jenna Gleisner
Designer: Michelle Sonnek

Photo Credits: itor/Shutterstock, cover; kazoka/Shutterstock, 1; Alexander Sviridov/Shutterstock, 3; Kondratuk Aleksei/Shutterstock, 4; Lee Rentz/Alamy, 5; Michael Patrick O'Neill/Alamy, 6-7; EcoPrint/Shutterstock, 8-9; Irh847/iStock, 10; NatureDiver/Shutterstock, 11; Ivan Kuzmin/imageBROKER/SuperStock, 12-13t; Simagart/Shutterstock, 12-13b; Fred Bavendam/Minden Pictures/SuperStock, 14-15; mastersky/Shutterstock, 16; tank200bar/Shutterstock, 17; Samlyn_Studio/iStock, 18-19tl; Oksana Maksymova/Shutterstock, 18-19tr; Luca Gialdini/iStock, 18-19bl; Damsea/Shutterstock, 18-19br; Jonathan Hernould/Shutterstock, 20-21; Process/Shutterstock, 23.

Printed in the United States of America at Corporate Graphics in North Mankato, Minnesota.

TABLE OF CONTENTS

CHAPTER 1
Shells and Claws..................................4

CHAPTER 2
Surviving in the Ocean........................10

CHAPTER 3
Kinds of Crabs...................................16

ACTIVITIES & TOOLS
Try This!..22
Glossary..23
Index...24
To Learn More..................................24

CHAPTER 1
SHELLS AND CLAWS

A crab walks sideways along the ocean floor. Why does it move this way? A crab's legs don't face forward like ours. They face the sides.

Crabs are **invertebrates**. Like other **crustaceans**, they don't have any bones. Hard outer shells protect their soft bodies.

shell

Crabs have five pairs of legs. Four pairs are used for walking. The front pair are called chelipeds. These have claws.

Crabs use their claws to dig. They use them for protection, too. Claws can cut, crush, and tear. They can also grip and carry things. Crabs move food to their mouths with their claws.

DID YOU KNOW?

Some crabs use their claws and legs to **communicate**. How? They rub them together to make sounds.

cheliped

claw

CHAPTER 1 7

eyestalk

Crabs can hide and still see their **predators**. How? Their eyes are on eyestalks. The stalks move. This lets crabs see all around. They can hide their bodies under sand, mud, or water. Their eyes peek out!

CHAPTER 1

TAKE A LOOK!

Two antennas touch, smell, and taste. They help crabs find food. What are a crab's other body parts called? Take a look!

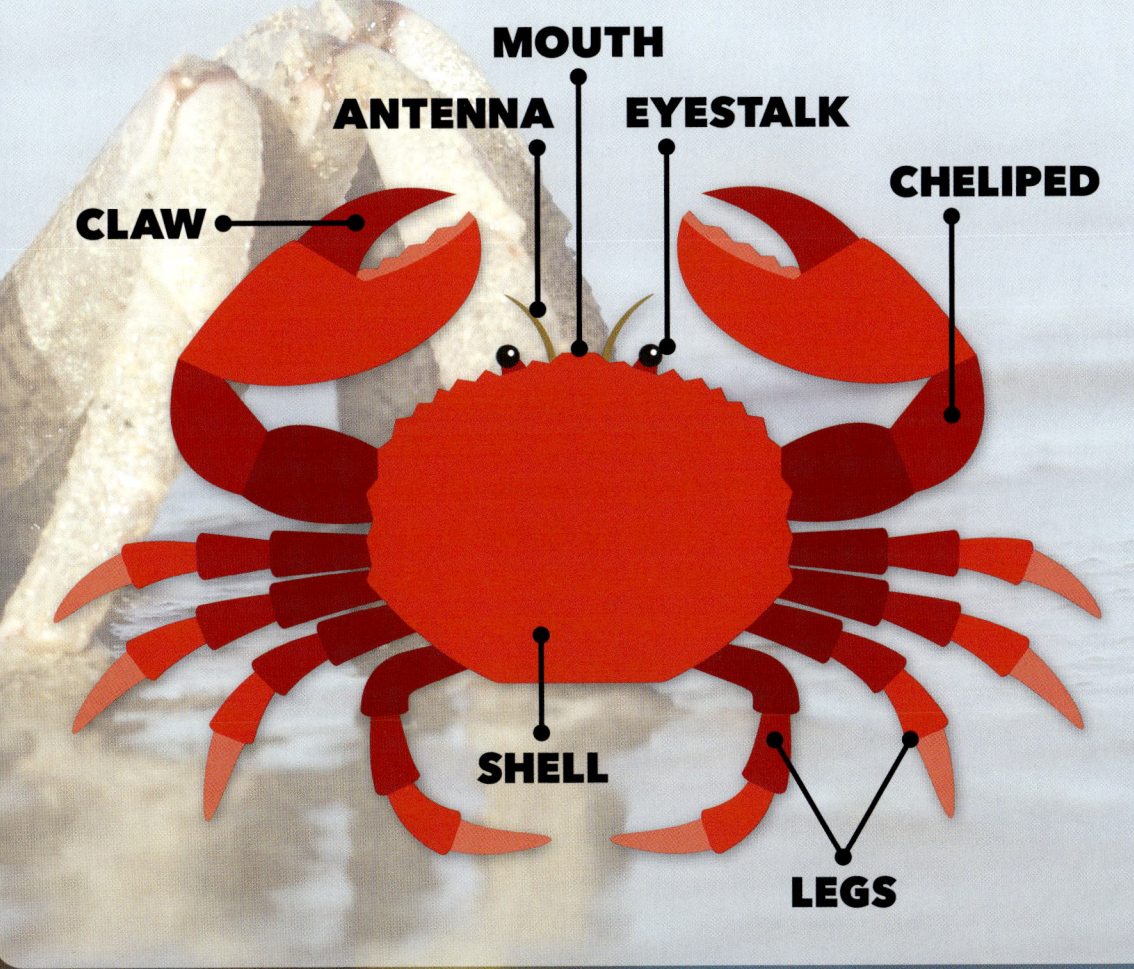

- CLAW
- ANTENNA
- MOUTH
- EYESTALK
- CHELIPED
- SHELL
- LEGS

CHAPTER 1 9

CHAPTER 2
SURVIVING IN THE OCEAN

Crabs have many predators. Birds and fish eat crabs. Octopuses, sea turtles, and humans do, too.

seaweed

Their shells can be good **camouflage**. They can blend in with sand, rocks, and **coral reefs**. Some crabs cover their shells in seaweed.

CHAPTER 2

Atlantic sand fiddler crab

pom-pom crab

sea anemone

Some crabs wave their claws to scare predators. The Atlantic sand fiddler crab does this. It has one very large claw.

The pom-pom crab carries sea anemones in its claws. Why? It uses them to sting predators. Look out!

DID YOU KNOW?

Crabs fight predators with their claws. Sometimes they fight one another, too. Why? They defend their **territories**. They may lose claws or legs in a fight. But they can grow back!

CHAPTER 2 13

Most crabs are **omnivores**. They eat **algae**, worms, clams, mussels, and more! They are also **scavengers**. This means they eat dead plants and animals they find.

CHAPTER 2

CHAPTER 3

KINDS OF CRABS

There are more than 6,000 **species** of crabs. They come in many sizes and colors. Pea crabs are one of the smallest. Some live in the shells of mussels and oysters. A pea crab's shell is less than one inch (2.5 centimeters) across.

Japanese spider crabs are the largest. They can weigh 44 pounds (20 kilograms). These crabs can live to be 100 years old!

blue crab

soft coral crab

orangutan crab

yellowline arrow crab

The blue crab has bright blue legs. The soft coral crab is colorful, too. It lives on bright coral, so its colors are good camouflage. The orangutan crab catches food in its thick hair. The yellowline arrow crab has long, skinny legs.

CHAPTER 3

Crabs live in every ocean. Some live in **tide pools**, marshes, or close to shore. Others live in deep, cold ocean waters.

Crabs are interesting sea creatures. Would you like to see one?

DID YOU KNOW?

Some crab species live in fresh water. Some can even live on land. But most at least visit water to **spawn**.

ACTIVITIES & TOOLS

TRY THIS!

CRAB WALK RELAY

See what it's like to walk like a crab in this fun relay race!

What You Need:
- an even number of friends or classmates
- an adult

❶ Gather a group of friends or classmates. Make sure you have an even number of people, including yourself.

❷ Split into two teams. The teams will compete in a relay race!

❸ Have an adult pick a start and finish line. Have each team line up behind the starting line.

❹ Have everyone get into crab walk position. Sit on the floor. Put your feet out in front of you, and bend your knees so your feet are flat on the floor. Place your hands behind you with your palms flat on the floor. Then push up so your body is in the air. Walk sideways.

❺ When everyone is ready, the adult can count down to start the race. Have the adult say, "Three, two, one . . . go!"

❻ Do the crab relay! When each person has completed their leg of the race, they will tag the next person in line.

❼ When it's over, discuss with your group whether the crab walk was difficult or easy. Do you think it is easier for crabs to walk this way? Why or why not?

GLOSSARY

algae: Small plants without roots or stems that grow mainly in water.

camouflage: A disguise or natural coloring that allows animals to hide by making them look like their surroundings.

communicate: To share information, ideas, or feelings with another.

coral reefs: Long lines of coral that lie in warm, shallow waters.

crustaceans: Types of ocean animals that have outer skeletons, such as lobsters, crabs, and shrimp.

invertebrates: Animals that do not have backbones.

omnivores: Animals that eat both plants and meat.

predators: Animals that hunt other animals for food.

scavengers: Animals that eat dead or decaying material.

spawn: To produce and release a large number of eggs.

species: One of the groups into which similar animals and plants are divided.

territories: Areas that animals claim and defend.

tide pools: Pools of water left behind when the ocean tide is low.

INDEX

bodies 5, 8
body parts 9
bones 5
camouflage 11, 19
chelipeds 6, 9
claws 6, 9, 13
communicate 6
coral reefs 11
eat 14
eyestalks 8, 9
fight 13
hide 8
land 20
legs 4, 6, 9, 13, 19
mouths 6, 9
ocean 4, 20
predators 8, 10, 13
seaweed 11
shells 5, 9, 11, 16
spawn 20
species 16, 20
territories 13
tide pools 20
walks 4, 6

TO LEARN MORE

Finding more information is as easy as 1, 2, 3.

❶ Go to www.factsurfer.com
❷ Enter "crabs" into the search box.
❸ Choose your book to see a list of websites.

24 ACTIVITIES & TOOLS